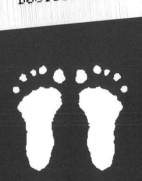

The BAREFOOT BOOK of
GIANTS, GHOSTS
AND GOBLINS

For Aidan and John-Michael — J. M.
For Laura — G. M.

Barefoot Collections
an imprint of
Barefoot Books Ltd
PO Box 95
Kingswood
Bristol
BS30 5BH

Text copyright © 1999 by John Matthews
Illustrations copyright © 1999 by Giovanni Manna

First published in Great Britain in 1999 by Barefoot Books Ltd

This book has been printed on 100% acid-free paper
The illustrations were prepared in china ink and watercolour
on 100% cotton 300gsm watercolour paper

Graphic design by Jennie Hoare, Bradford on Avon
Typeset in Bembo 14pt
Colour separation by Unifoto, Cape Town
Printed and bound in Hong Kong by South China Printing Co. (1988) Ltd.

ISBN 1 902283 26 0

British Cataloguing-in-Publication Data:
a catalogue record for this book is available from the British Library

1 3 5 7 9 8 6 4 2

The BAREFOOT BOOK of
GIANTS, GHOSTS AND GOBLINS

Traditional Tales from Around the World

Retold by
JOHN MATTHEWS

Illustrated by
GIOVANNI MANNA

BAREFOOT BOOKS
BATH

Contents

Contents

Introduction

IN FOLK-TALES AND MYTHS the world over, giants, ghosts and goblins are just about the favourite candidates for the role of opponent or challenger to the main character. Whenever the hero has to encounter something difficult, something more dangerous than any challenge he has met before, you can be sure that he will run into one or more of these three beings.

Giants, ghosts and goblins always have their own distinctive qualities. Giants can be comical as well as scary, like the one in the story of 'Oona and the Giant', or they can be plain horrible, like 'The Giant with No Heart in His Body'. Ghosts, despite being generally thought of as terrifying, can also be helpful, as in the Chinese story 'The Drinking Companions', or even a little sad like the Cheyenne ghost with two faces, who falls in love with a human girl. Goblins, on the other hand, are nearly always nasty, cruel and sly — though in this collection we meet one in 'The Goblin, the Grocer and the Student' who is really rather nice and cares much more about the important things in life than does the grocer. Even the fierce and terrible Bunyip from Australia seems justified in behaving the way she does and punishing the lazy men.

What is most noticeable about all three kinds of being is that they make things happen. In these stories there would be no adventures without them. They force the heroes and heroines to grow and learn, which is what makes these folk-tales so perennially enjoyable and relevant to our own lives.

As always with a collection of this kind, my hardest task as compiler was deciding what to put in and what to leave out. In the end I chose to retell stories I have always liked from as many parts of the world as

possible. I make no secret of the fact that 'Little Oonyani' and 'A-Man-Among-Men' are two of my personal favourites — 'Little Oonyani' because it seems to me to embody the most surreal and magical aspects of folk-tale, 'A-Man-Among-Men' because it says so much about real people with real feelings, who are often given to bragging about their strength or other qualities, but who seldom measure up to their boastful accounts of themselves.

Another priority for me was to select stories that show the different ways in which people relate to the giants, ghosts and goblins of their own folk-history. Thus the Irish and the Scots have a wonderfully casual, natural way of dealing with giants and goblins, as though they are to be met with every day — which perhaps they are! The Native American people and the Aboriginal race of Australia both have a much more nervous attitude towards such beings, experiencing them as being tricky and pernicious in their ways. In China, as we see in 'The Drinking Companions', ghosts are perceived as bringing good as well as bad fortune. The Eastern belief in the continuing power of their ancestors contributes to this, and makes for a wonderful story of trust, and of friendship stretching down the years. The Scandinavian tales, 'The Giant with No Heart in His Body' and 'The Goblin, the Grocer and the Student', reflect a powerful and sometimes dark aspect of these regions, whose folklore derives very clearly from the old Norse myths of the gods.

One of the rewards about doing a collection like this is to see the stories brought to life by new and exciting pictures. I would like to pay tribute here to Giovanni Manna, whose paintings capture the spirit of these old tales in a truly magical fashion. I hope everyone who has ever wondered about giants and goblins, or shivered at a ghostly tale, will enjoy this new collection of stories as much as I have enjoyed watching them come to life.

John Matthews
Oxford

The Giant with No Heart in His Body

Norwegian

There was once a king who had seven sons whom he loved very much. Indeed, he loved them so much that he always had to have at least one of them by his side. And so, when they were grown into handsome young men and wanted to set out in search of suitable princesses, the king gave all of them permission to go except one — the youngest, who was called Ashpattle.

The king could not bear to be without at least one of his sons, so he kept Ashpattle at home and made the older princes promise to bring back a bride for their younger brother.

Well, the six princes went searching through all the neighbouring kingdoms until they found a king who had six daughters, and every one of them as beautiful as the day. And the six princes wooed the six princesses, and won them. Then they set off for home, having quite forgotten to bring a seventh princess for Ashpattle.

On the way they passed a huge, dark castle, which was the home of a fearsome giant, who just happened to be looking out of the window at the time. Furious that anyone dared to trespass on his lands, the giant turned all six princes and all six princesses to stone. And there they stood.

Time passed and the king grew more anxious every day that his sons did not return. 'Thank goodness I didn't let you go as well,' he said to Ashpattle.

'As it happens,' answered the prince, 'I was just thinking of going to look for my brothers.'

'No, no, no!' cried the king. 'I will lose you as well!'

But Ashpattle insisted. He nagged and nagged until the king finally gave in. But having spent a fortune equipping the other princes with fine clothes and magnificent horses, he had nothing left to give to his youngest child but a poor suit and a broken-down old horse. Ashpattle didn't mind at all. 'Don't worry, Father,' he said as he left. 'I shall return. And who knows, I may bring my brothers back as well.'

So Ashpattle set out along the road, and he had not gone very far before he saw a raven lying in the road. The bird was so weak with hunger that it could not even get out of the way. When it saw the prince, it called out to him: 'Please spare me a little food. If you do, I promise to help you when you most need it.'

'I don't know about that,' said Ashpattle, 'but you can have some of my food anyway.'

Ashpattle went on his way, and in a little while he came to a river. On the bank was a huge salmon, which had become stranded. When it saw the prince, it called out to him: 'Help me get back into the water. If you do, I promise to help you when you are most in need.'

'I don't know about that,' said Ashpattle, 'but I'll help you anyway.' And he gathered up the fish in his arms and tossed it back into the water. Then he went on his way.

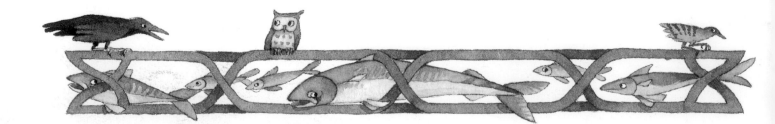

For days and weeks Ashpattle travelled on without a sign of his brothers. In the end his broken-down old horse fell dead beneath him. As he stood by the road, wondering how he was going to get along, a wolf came crawling towards him.

It was so weak and thin that it looked as though a puff of wind would blow it away. 'Please,' it said to the prince. 'Give me your horse. I haven't eaten anything for a year, and I'm starving. If you do this for me, I shall help you find your brothers.'

'I don't know about that,' said Ashpattle, 'but you are welcome to whatever meat you can get off my poor old horse.' So the wolf set to and when it had finished it was so much stronger that it offered to carry Ashpattle on its back. The prince put his saddle on its back and a bit in its mouth and off they sped, much faster than the poor old horse had ever gone. Soon they arrived at the giant's castle, and Ashpattle saw the twelve lumps of stone standing beside the road.

'Those are your brothers and the six princesses they were bringing home with them,' said the wolf. 'If you want to save them you have to go in and confront the giant.'

'But won't he kill me?' said Ashpattle.

'Well, he might,' said the wolf. 'But inside there is a princess who knows all about the giant and his ways. She will help you.'

So Ashpattle went up to the door of the castle and knocked. The door was opened by the most beautiful girl he had ever seen. 'Go away quickly,' she cried. 'This castle belongs to a giant. If he comes home and finds you here, he will certainly kill you.'

'Those are my brothers outside, turned to stone,' said Ashpattle. 'Now that I'm here I must do the best I can to rescue them.' And he added, 'Maybe I can save you as well.'

The princess blushed. 'Well,' she said, 'we must just do the best we can. Go and hide under the bed, and be sure to listen carefully to everything you hear.'

No sooner had Ashpattle hidden himself than the giant came home. He sniffed the air. 'There's a terrible smell of human flesh in here,' he bellowed.

'Oh,' said the princess. 'A magpie flew over the castle this afternoon and dropped a human bone down the chimney. I threw it out at once, but the smell does take time to go.'

The giant said no more and soon it was time for bed. The princess lay down next to the giant. After a while she said: 'There was something I wanted to ask you, but I'm too afraid.'

'What is it?' asked the giant.

'Well,' said the princess. 'I know you don't carry your heart with you. I was just wondering where you kept it.'

'That's nothing to do with you,' said the giant. 'But if you must know, it's under the stone slab in front of the door.'

'Ah, ha!' thought Ashpattle, who was, of course, still hidden under the bed. 'Now I know what to do.'

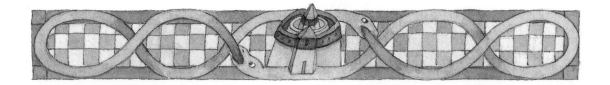

In the morning the giant went off in search of prey. As soon as he was out of sight, Ashpattle and the princess started digging up the stone slab in front of the door in search of the heart. They dug and dug until finally they realised that the giant had lied.

'You had better hide under the bed again tonight,' said the princess. 'He won't fool me again.' Then she picked all the prettiest flowers she could find and strewed them over the doorstep.

Soon the giant came home. 'There's still a terrible smell of human flesh around here,' he said suspiciously.

'Oh,' said the princess. 'That magpie came by again and it dropped another human bone down the chimney. I got rid of it as quickly as possible, but the smell does linger.'

The giant said nothing for a while, then he asked who had been strewing flowers all over the doorstep.

14

'That was me,' said the princess. 'Since I know your heart is under there I wanted to make it nice.'

'Well, you needn't have bothered,' said the giant. 'My heart isn't there at all.'

'Oh,' said the princess, and later on when they were lying side by side — and Ashpattle was again hidden under the bed — she said: 'If your heart isn't under the doorstep, where is it?'

'In that cupboard up there on the wall,' said the giant. 'Now stop asking questions and go to sleep.'

Next day, when the giant had left in search of food, Ashpattle and the princess searched the cupboard for the heart. Once again they found nothing.

The princess declared: 'Well, we shall just have to try again.' Then she got garlands and hung them all around the cupboard.

When the giant came home he sniffed and roared that there was still a horrible smell of human flesh in the house. 'I'm sorry,' the princess said. 'That magpie came by again and dropped another bone down the chimney. I did my best to get rid of the smell, but it takes a long time to go away.'

'Humph!' said the giant. 'Why are there garlands all round my cupboard?'

'Ah,' said the princess. 'Since your heart is in there I wanted to make it as nice as I could.'

'You needn't have bothered,' the giant grumbled. 'It's not in there at all. You can never know where my heart is.'

'Oh dear,' said the princess. 'If only I knew where it was I should be so happy.'

'Well,' the giant said reluctantly. 'Since you have been so nice to me lately, I'll tell you. Far away from here is an island. On the island is a tower, and in the tower there is a well. In the well swims a duck. Inside the duck is an egg and inside the egg is my heart. So you see, you could never get to it, even if you tried.'

Under the bed, Ashpattle ground his teeth. 'How am I going to find the giant's heart?' he wondered.

Next morning, the giant once again left the castle early in search of a meal. When he had gone, Ashpattle bade farewell to the princess. 'I only wish I knew where I was going,' he said. 'But I have to try anyway.'

Outside the castle he found the wolf waiting. When it heard about the giant's heart, it said, 'I know the way. Jump on my back and I'll take you there.'

Off they sped, faster than the wind, but it still took them three days to reach the lake. Ashpattle stood at the edge of the water, looking across at the island. 'How am I going to get across?' he wondered.

'I'll take you,' said the wolf. 'Have courage.' Then, with the prince on his back, he swam across to the island.

There, at the centre, stood the tower. It had one door and the key was hanging on the wall far too high up for Ashpattle to reach.

'Now what shall I do?' said the prince.

'You must call the raven,' answered the wolf.

Ashpattle did so, and in a few moments the raven landed in an untidy bundle of feathers at his feet. The prince explained his problem and the bird flew up at once and fetched the key. Ashpattle went inside and here, just as the giant had said, was the well with the duck swimming about in it.

Ashpattle reached in and seized the duck, but in its fright it dropped the egg, which sank beneath the murky waters of the well.

'Now what shall I do?' said Ashpattle.

'You must call the salmon,' said the wolf.

Ashpattle did so, and in less than a minute the salmon rose up to the top of the well.

The prince explained his problem and at once the salmon swam down and returned with the egg. 'Now,' said the wolf. 'Squeeze the egg.'

Ashpattle squeezed, and even though they were hundreds of miles away, they heard the giant scream.

Holding the egg, Ashpattle jumped on to the wolf's back and away they sped, faster than the wind. Soon they were back at the giant's castle, and there Ashpattle squeezed the egg even harder.

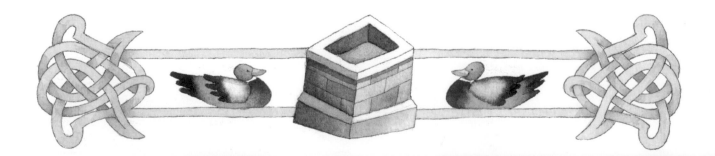

With a terrible cry, the giant came bursting out of the castle. He fell at the prince's feet and begged to be spared. 'Turn my brothers and their brides back from stone,' demanded Ashpattle. The giant was eager to do as he asked, and in a moment the six princes and the six princesses stood blinking in the light of day.

'Now,' whispered the wolf, 'squeeze the egg to pieces.'

Ashpattle squeezed the egg until it was quite flat, and the giant fell down and burst into a hundred pieces.

After that, everything went very well for everyone. Ashpattle and his brothers and the six princesses, and, of course, the princess from the giant's castle, went home together and they all got married. Ashpattle rewarded the wolf, the raven and the salmon by telling them to visit him whenever they wanted and to eat as much as they liked. The king was delighted to have all his sons home again, and gave the place of honour at the top of the table to Ashpattle and his bride. Then they began a grand celebration, and if they haven't finished, they are at it still.

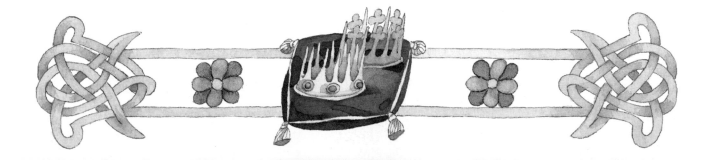

The Ghost with Two Faces

Cheyenne – North American

There was once a ghost who was very tall. He had long arms and even longer legs. But the strangest thing about him was that he had two faces, one looking back and the other looking forward. In spite of this, he wasn't an evil or horrible ghost. In fact, he was really quite nice — for a ghost, that is.

One day the ghost decided that he must get married, and so he set out in search of a wife. He went striding all over the place, but he couldn't find a girl who would marry him — not surprisingly, since he was a ghost. He kept on looking, however, and one day he saw a tipi standing all alone in the middle of the prairie.

The ghost hid behind a hill and watched. He saw that there were three people living in the tipi — a man and his wife and their beautiful daughter. When he saw her, the ghost fell in love with her at once and, of course, wanted to marry her. But he knew by now

that whenever he appeared people ran off screaming. So instead of going up to the tipi and announcing himself, he went off and hunted all day long until he had a huge heap of game. He took this back to the tipi and laid it outside the door.

In the morning the family came out and found all the meat — far more than they could ever eat themselves. The same thing happened the next day, and the day after that.

'I must find out who's doing this,' said the father.

That night he dug a hole in the earth outside the tipi and hid himself in it. Soon he saw the ghost coming, striding across the earth with his huge long legs and his two faces. He stopped beside the tipi and laid down a fresh load of game, then he ran off quickly.

Trembling with fear, the man got out of the hole and went to tell his wife and daughter what he had seen.

'We must get away before that terrible monster comes back again,' said his wife.

So they packed up the tipi and hurried away as swiftly as they could.

Next morning, the ghost came by with his offerings and saw that they had gone. He chased after them and, of course, with his long legs and four pairs of eyes, he soon saw and caught up with them.

'Stop! Wait!' he shouted. 'I mean you no harm. Let's sit down and talk.'

Well, there wasn't much else the family could do. So they stopped and sat down with the ghost, though they were all trembling with fright at the sight of his two faces.

'It was kind of you to leave all that food,' said the father.

'Well, you see,' said the ghost, 'I'm in love with your daughter. In fact, I want to marry her.'

The man looked at his wife and the wife looked at the man and they both looked at their daughter. All three knew that nothing in the world would make her marry the ghost — after all, who wants a husband three times taller than herself and with two faces? But the man was cunning. He smiled at the ghost.

'What a wonderful offer,' he said. 'We have seen what a great
hunter you are, and very kind as well. I can't think of anyone I'd
rather give my daughter to. And, of course, you know the custom of
my people in such cases.'

'What custom is that?' asked the ghost.

'We always play hide-the-plum-pit,' said the father. 'If the suitor
wins, he gets to marry the girl; if not, he gives us a gift.'

'I've never heard of that custom,' said the ghost, doubtfully.

'Oh, we've had it since the beginning of time,' said the man. 'If
we don't follow it, terrible things will happen to us all.'

'I suppose we'd better play, then,' said the ghost.

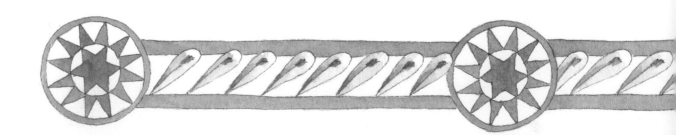

What he didn't know was that the girl's father was the best hide-the-plum-pit player in all the world. In fact, he had never been beaten, and wasn't this time. He beat the ghost every time, and even gave him several extra chances to be fair. But in the end the ghost admitted defeat.

'What gift would you like?' he asked sadly.

'Well,' said the father. 'I think you could just go on bringing us meat but maybe every other day.'

The ghost kept his word. Every other day, for as long as the family lived and even after the girl was married, he brought them food. But whether or not he ever found a wife, I've not heard.

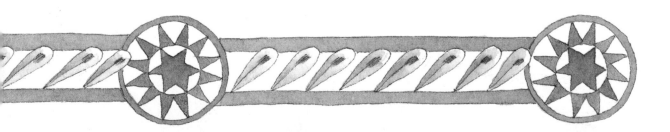

The Bunyip

Australian

There was once a group of young hunters who went out to collect food for their families. They headed for the only watering-place in the area, a deep, dark pool surrounded by rushes and full of tasty eels. They took a while to get there because they liked to stop and run races and practise throwing their spears.

When they got to the watering-place, they found that the summer sun had shrunk it to a few muddy puddles. The hunters began to weave a basket from the rushes, and were about to start collecting some of the delicious bulrush roots from beneath the mud, when one of them suddenly said loudly, 'Why are we doing this? It's really work for women. Let's leave it and go fishing for eels instead.'

All the rest thought this was a wonderful idea, and they took out their fishing-lines and looked for something to use as bait. Most used worms, but one of them had a piece of raw meat in his skin

wallet and, without telling anyone else, he used a piece of that, thinking that he would get a bigger catch.

For a time they all sat about in the hot sun, casting their lines into the water, but not one of them had a bite, and as the sun sank lower and lower in the sky it looked as though they would have to go home empty-handed, with not even a basket of roots to show for their day out.

Then the youth who had used meat for bait felt a tug on his line. Eagerly he began to pull it in, but whatever it was that he had caught was so heavy that he was almost pulled into the water himself. 'Hey! Come and help me!' he called out to his friends, and they held on to one another, and together they pulled on the line.

Out came the strangest-looking creature you ever saw, a cross between a calf and a seal, with huge eyes and a fish tail.

The hunters gathered round and looked at the creature, and they began to tremble, because they knew what it was at once — the cub of the terrible monster called the Bunyip, which was believed to live around there.

'Quickly, throw it back!' they whispered. But the youth who had caught it shook his head. 'This is the best catch I ever had,' he declared. 'I promised my sweetheart I would bring back enough meat for her father's table to last three days. This will do very nicely.'

At that moment there came a horrible roar, and the Bunyip herself rose out of the water, her great horns gleaming and her great round saucer-eyes glaring with fury at the men who had dared to steal her cub.

But, despite his fear, the young man was determined to hold on to his catch. He slung the whimpering cub across his back and ran off as fast as he could, followed by his fellows.

They ran and ran and soon the roars of the Bunyip faded away behind them. They began to slow down, and even laughed among themselves at their cleverness in escaping.

Then they heard a rushing sound behind them and, looking back, saw a raging wall of water coming towards them. There wasn't a cloud in the sky, but still the water went on rising. The young men yelled with fear and ran on again until they reached the higher ground overlooking the great plain where the watering-hole lay.

Then they looked back again, and saw to their terror that the water was still rising, covering all the dry land between them and the Bunyip's hole.

On they flew, as fast as they could run, and still the one who had caught the little Bunyip carried it across his back.

At last, they reached the camp where they lived, and fell into the middle of their surprised families, gasping out just two words, 'The Water! The Water!'

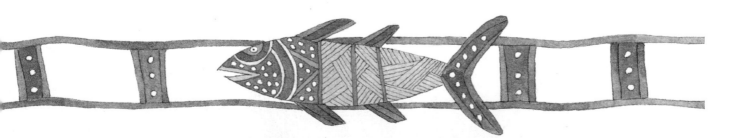

Everyone looked in the direction of the Bunyip's hole and saw the water slowly advancing towards them. The boy who had caught the little Bunyip grabbed his sweetheart. 'Quickly,' he said. 'Let's climb that tree over there, then we'll be safe.'

But even as he spoke he felt something strange about his feet. Looking down, he saw that they had turned into scaly bird-claws. He turned to the girl beside him, but saw only a huge black bird. He looked at his friends, but saw only more birds. He put up his hands to cover his face, but they were not his hands any more, only the tips of black wing-feathers. He tried to speak, but the only sound that came from his throat was a strange hissing cry. He looked down into the water, and saw only the reflection of a great, black swan — one of many that bobbed on the water.

In another moment the Bunyip arrived, in search of her cub. The swans all hissed and moved as far away as they could. The Bunyip waited for her cub to climb on to her back, then swam off back to her hole, with a last roar. Slowly the waters shrank back until there was not a sign that they had ever been, save for a flock of black swans flapping and hissing to each other.

It is said that the people never did recover their own shapes, but remained swans for ever. And it is said that if you listen to them at night, you can hear the swans talking amongst themselves in a strange language.

No one saw the Bunyip again, though it is said that she still lives at the bottom of her deep, dark, watering-hole, surrounded by treasures. But no one dares to go and look for them.

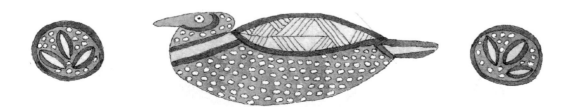

Oona and the Giant

Irish

A long time ago, Ireland was full of giants. They were all great rivals, and whenever they met they would pummel and punch each other until one of them gave up or ran away. But everyone agreed that the mightiest giant of all was Cuchulainn. He had never been beaten himself, and had managed to knock out just about every other giant in the land.

There was just one that he hadn't fought, and that was Fionn mac Cool. The reason for this was that Fionn had the ability to see what was going on anywhere in the world. All he had to do was to put his left thumb into his mouth and suck it — and at once he knew what had happened, what was happening, and what would happen. That way he managed to avoid meeting up with Cuchulainn at all, since whenever he saw the giant coming he simply ran off and hid until Cuchulainn had taken himself off again.

This annoyed Cuchulainn. He wanted to be known as the biggest, fiercest, ugliest giant in all Ireland, but as long as he hadn't fought Fionn, there was always a chance — just a chance — that he might be beaten.

So one day Cuchulainn set off for the mountain where Fionn lived. Fionn had built his house high up on the mountain — some people said so that he could see other giants coming and hide from them. As Cuchulainn was climbing up the steep cliffs, Fionn looked out of the window and saw him.

'Oh dear!' he cried. 'That dreadful Cuchulainn is coming! He's bound to catch me this time.'

Now, Fionn had a wife named Oona, who was as clever as she was kind, and as beautiful as she was skilled. 'How long before he arrives?' she asked.

Fionn put his thumb into his mouth. 'At about three o'clock. And he means to squash me as flat as a cow-pat. Whatever shall I do?'

'Hush, now,' said Oona. 'Just do what I say and everything will work out just fine.'

Right away, Oona began

baking a batch of huge cakes. Three of them she made just as usual, but she put huge stones into the other three. When they were done, she arranged them on two shelves — the three ordinary cakes on the top shelf and the three with the stones on the bottom. Then she told Fionn to get into a big wicker cradle, and she wrapped him round in a big blanket and put a lace cape on his huge head. 'Now just you stay there and pretend to be a baby,' she said. 'You can suck your thumb and you'll know exactly what I'm thinking and what I want you to do. Just tell me one thing — where does this giant keep his strength?'

'Why, in the middle finger of his right hand,' said Fionn.

Oona nodded, then she sat down in her rocking-chair and waited for Cuchulainn to arrive.

At exactly three o'clock he pounded on the door.

Fionn pulled the blanket over his head and trembled with fear, but Oona threw open the door.

'Is this the house of Fionn mac Cool?' thundered Cuchulainn.

'It is,' answered Oona. 'Come in and sit you down.'

So Cuchulainn came in and sat himself down in Fionn's chair and looked around.

'That's a fine baby you have there,' he said. 'Would his father be at home by any chance?'

'I'm afraid not,' said Oona. 'He said something about going to catch some little fellow called Cuchulainn. I'm sure he won't be long.'

'I'm Cuchulainn,' growled the giant. 'I've been trying to catch up with your husband for ages, but he always manages to give me the slip.'

'So you're Cuchulainn,' said Oona. 'Well, you still have time to get away before Fionn comes home.'

'*Me* run away from *him*!' shouted Cuchulainn. 'It's *him* that always runs away from *me*!'

'I think you've got it wrong,' said Oona. 'Have you seen my husband? He's as hard as rock and as swift as the wind.' She smiled. 'Oh, and by the way, could you turn the house around, the wind is shifting.'

'Turn the house around!' said Cuchulainn.

'That's what Fionn always does when the wind blows from the east,' said Oona.

Cuchulainn went outside, shook his head a few times, then clicked the middle finger of his right hand three times. Then he seized the house around the middle and turned it right round.

Inside, Fionn's teeth chattered with fright, but Oona merely hushed him, and when Cuchulainn came inside thanked him as though he had just done the most ordinary thing. Then she said, 'The weather is so dry and I am always needing water. Could you go and fill this jug for me? Then we can have a cup of tea while you wait for Fionn to come home.'

'Where shall I go to get water hereabouts?' said Cuchulainn.

Oona pointed to a nearby hill. 'You see that stone on top of yonder hill? Whenever we need water, Fionn goes up there and takes that little rock out of the ground and fills the jug from the stream that rises underneath.'

Cuchulainn dutifully went out and climbed the hill. At the top he saw that the stone was three times as tall as himself and must have weighed several tons. Clicking the middle finger of his right hand nine times, he put his arms about the rock and lifted it clean out of the ground. A stream gushed out and roared away down the mountainside, and Cuchulainn soon had a jug full of water.

Oona made a large pot of tea and offered Cuchulainn one of the special cakes in which she had hidden a stone. The giant took one bite and howled. He spat out a huge tooth.

'What kind of cake is this?' he cried. 'It's as hard as stone.'

'That's Fionn's favourite cake,' said Oona. 'Even the baby loves it. But maybe it's too much for you. Here, try this one, it's a bit softer.' And she gave him another of the stony cakes.

Cuchulainn took a huge bite and spat out two teeth with a yell of pain.

'Hush now,' said Oona. 'You'll wake the baby.'

At that moment Fionn sucked his thumb and at once he knew what Oona wanted him to do. He let out the loudest shout ever heard in that part of Ireland. Cuchulainn jumped up and put his hands over his ears.

'My, but that baby has a mighty pair of lungs,' he said.

'Oh, you should hear his father,' said Oona. 'When he shouts, you can hear him in Africa.'

Cuchulainn began to feel uneasy. The more he heard about Fionn mac Cool the less he liked the sound of him. At that moment Fionn, who was sucking his thumb again, opened his mouth wide and yelled 'CAKE!' at the top of his lungs.

'There now,' said Oona, and handed him a cake from the top shelf. 'Just you eat that.'

Cuchulainn watched in horror as the baby ate every last crumb of the cake.

'I think I'll be going,' he said. 'Tell your husband I'm sorry I missed him and congratulations to you both on a bonny baby.'

'Oh, he's a wonderful child,' said Oona. 'Come and take a proper look.' She pulled back the blanket and Fionn yelled and kicked his legs in the air for all he was worth.

'What a pair of legs he has on him,' said Cuchulainn.

'Yes, and his teeth are coming through nicely,' said Oona. 'Just you feel them.'

Thinking he would please her and then make his escape before her terrible husband came home, Cuchulainn put his hand into the baby's mouth.

Quick as a flash, Fionn bit off the middle finger. Cuchulainn howled so loudly that he could be heard in Timbuktu. Then, as his strength began to ebb, he began to get smaller. He shrank until he was even smaller than the cakes that Oona had made. Fionn and his wife looked down at the little giant and smiled. Cuchulainn took one look at them and fled out of the house and away down the mountain. What happened to him after that I can't say, because he was never seen or heard of again in Ireland.

As for Fionn mac Cool, he just thanked his clever wife and ate another of her fine cakes.

The Drinking Companions

Chinese

A long time ago in the country of China, a farmer named Hsu had a house outside the walls of the city of Tzu. Every night he liked to go fishing in the nearby river, where he always seemed to catch more than anyone else. He always took along a bottle of wine to drink, but before he had any himself he would pour some into the river in honour of those who had drowned in its swiftly rushing waters.

One day, when he was sitting on the riverbank waiting for a bite, a young man came along. For some time he paced up and down as if waiting for something. Finally, Hsu called out to him and asked if he would like to share some of his wine. The young man readily agreed, and they sat side by side and shared the drink, but it was a disappointing night for fishing, and Hsu wasn't getting a single bite. At last the young man said, 'Let me go downstream and see if I can chase some fish along this way.'

He went off so quickly that Hsu could have sworn that he was flying, and in a few moments he heard a lot of splashing in the water as a number of fish swam into view. Eagerly, Hsu threw his line in and in no time at all he had a pile of fish on the riverbank beside him.

'Thank you,' he said to the young man. 'Won't you please take some of my fish?'

The young man declined, saying, 'I have often shared your fine wine. This was but a small assistance in return. But, if you don't mind, I have enjoyed myself so much that I'd like to come here again and share your company.'

'Since we only met tonight,' said Hsu, 'I don't see how you can have shared my wine before. But you're welcome to join me whenever you like.' And he asked the young man his name.

'You may call me Liu-Lang, or Sixth-Born,' he said.

Next night they met again, and again shared a bottle of wine. And, as he had done the night before, the young man went some way downstream and sent many fish up to where Hsu was waiting.

This went on for almost a year, and the two became fast friends. Then one evening Liu-Lang was unusually silent. 'Is anything wrong?' asked Hsu.

'I'm afraid this will be the last night we spend together.'

'Why should that be?' asked Hsu, with concern. 'Are you sick?'

Several times the young man began to speak and stopped. At last, he said, 'You must promise not to be afraid. You see, I am a ghost. I fell into the river when I had drunk too much. I've been here ever since, waiting to move on. The reason you always caught more fish here than anyone else is because I have been sending the fish down to you as a thanks for all the libations of wine you gave me. Now it is time for me to go on my way.'

At first, Hsu was very frightened, but he thought of all the pleasant evenings he had spent with Liu-Lang and his fears went away. 'One thing I don't understand,' he said. 'Why do you have to go now?'

'Tomorrow I am going to be replaced,' said Liu-Lang. 'A woman will fall into the river just over there and drown. Her ghost will take my place and I shall be reborn as someone else.'

'Surely that is a cause for happiness,' said Hsu. And the two of them sat down side by side to share a bottle of wine for the very last time.

Next day, Hsu decided to hide by the river and watch what happened. Soon a woman came along with a baby in her arms. As she reached the riverbank she slipped and fell in. She managed to toss the baby on to the bank, but she herself began to sink and cry out for help.

Hsu had difficulty in stopping himself from rushing to her aid, but he remembered what Liu-Lang had said and watched to see what would happen.

At last the woman managed to pull herself out of the river. She picked up her baby and ran off. Hsu was left wondering whether his old friend had been telling the truth.

That night he went to his usual spot on the riverbank, and there he found Liu-Lang.

'I don't understand,' said Hsu.

'Well, you see,' said Liu-Lang, 'that woman was meant to take my place, but when I saw that she had a baby I couldn't bear to let it happen. So I pushed her out of the water. Anyway, it means that you and I can go on meeting here for a bit longer.'

Hsu was very happy to hear this, though he felt sorry for his friend.

A few days later Liu-Lang came full of excitement and told him that he was to move on after all.

'It seems the gods decided I had done a kind thing by letting the woman live,' he said. 'So instead of being reborn I am going to become a local god in the township of Wu in the province of Chuyuan. Be sure you come and visit me there, and never mind the distance. Just come anyway.'

Now, the province of Chuyuan was hundreds of miles away, but Hsu was determined to go and visit his old friend. So he put his affairs in order and set out, despite the fact that everyone else thought he was mad.

His journey was long, but he finally reached the township of Wu and took a room in the local hostel. There he asked the way to the temple.

'Ah,' said his host. 'Would your name be Hsu, by any chance?'

'Why, yes,' replied Hsu, in astonishment. 'How did you know?'

But the host had already hurried off, and when he returned the whole township was with him.

Hsu was more amazed than ever, but the people explained to him that they had all had the same dream a few nights before in which their local god told them that a good friend of his called Hsu was coming to stay, and that they should all help in any way they could with his travelling expenses.

Hsu went to the temple and prayed aloud to his old friend before the little shrine in his honour. 'Scarcely a day has passed without my thinking of you,' he said. 'And now here I am and you send people

to meet me in such a wonderful way. I am sorry that I did not bring a proper gift, but I would be glad to share this bottle of wine with you.' And, with that, he placed the bottle in the little shrine.

That night he dreamed of Liu-Lang, who thanked him for coming so far to see him. 'I hope we shall meet again one day,' he said. 'Meanwhile, when you get home, you will find that things will have got better for you.'

Hsu remained in the township of Wu for a few days more, and when he left he had all sorts of gifts given to him by the towns-people in honour of their god. As Hsu set out, a small whirlwind accompanied him for the first few miles. Then Hsu stopped and said, 'Don't bother coming any further, Liu-Lang. I'm sure you have many good things to do for the people in your care. Goodbye.'

The whirlwind hovered by him for a time, then vanished. Hsu went on with his long journey, and when he arrived at his old home, he found that Liu-Lang's words were true. Everything went well for him, and he soon became rich and comfortable. He never forgot his old friend, and nearly every night he went to the river and poured out some wine to the ghosts of those who had died in its fierce waters.

The Goblin, the Grocer
and the Student

Danish

There was once a grocer who had a goblin living in the basement. The goblin stayed there because every Christmas the grocer would put out a dish of cream and some jam, which he loved more than anything and, as everyone knows, if you give a goblin the things he likes most he will always be your friend.

In the attic at the top of the grocer's house lived a poor student, who had nothing in the world. One day he went downstairs to buy some bread and cheese from the grocer. On the way out he noticed that the cheese was wrapped up in a page torn from an old book.

'This is the most wonderful poetry,' he said. 'How can you use it to wrap cheese!'

'Oh, that!' said the grocer. 'There's more over there. An old woman paid me for some coffee with that book.' He rubbed his hands. 'If you want to give me tuppence you can have it.'

The student hesitated. 'It would be a shame to leave the book to be torn up, and I can eat my bread without cheese,' he said. 'You may be a clever man when it comes to business,' he added, 'but you know as much about poetry as that old biscuit-barrel over there.'

Now it happened that the goblin was listening and when he overheard this he was angry. He liked the grocer, who always gave him cream and jam at Christmas, and the student seemed to him no more than a lazybones, who spent all day up in his attic reading.

Later that night, when the shop was closed, the goblin came up from the basement and spoke to the old biscuit-barrel. 'Is it true,' he asked, 'that you know nothing about poetry?'

'Not at all,' replied the biscuit-barrel. 'The grocer often throws old newspapers into me and I read them all. There's lots of poetry in them.'

The goblin went around the shop asking everything if they knew about poetry. He asked the scales, the meat-grinder, the coffee-mill and the butter-cask, and every one of them said that it knew something about poetry.

'Now I shall tell that student that the grocer knows lots about poetry!' said the goblin, and he tiptoed upstairs to the attic. There he saw a bright light shining out from under the student's door. He peered through the keyhole into the room. There sat the student, bent over the old book he had got from the grocer.

But something amazing was happening. Out of the book shone a ray of light that shaped itself into a huge tree. The tree was covered in blossoms, and every blossom had the face of a beautiful girl. It had fruit on it as well, and the fruit glowed like stars! The most marvellous music filled the room and that, too, seemed to come from the tree.

The goblin stared. Never in his life had he seen or heard anything so beautiful. It was so beautiful it made him want to cry. He remained outside the student's door until the light went out and the student went to sleep. Even then, the goblin could hear gentle music like a lullaby. 'This is amazing,' he said to himself. 'I think I'll stay with the

student.' Then he thought again and sighed. 'But the student has no cream or jam!' he thought, remembering what the grocer gave him every Christmas. So the goblin crept off back to his home in the cellar. But every night after that he used to tiptoe upstairs and stand outside the student's door, listening to the music and peeping through the keyhole to see the wonderful tree.

Then, one night, there came a loud banging on the door of the shop and cries of 'Fire! Fire!' Everyone woke up and ran about looking for their most precious things to save. The grocer ran for his money, his wife for her jewels, but the goblin ran upstairs and into

the student's room. The student was looking out of the window at the burning houses across the street. But the goblin had no doubt at all what was the most valuable item in the house. It was the book!

There it was, lying on the table. The goblin grabbed it and hid it in his red cap. Then he sprang up the chimney and sat on the roof, watching the houses burn all along the other side of the street.

Soon the fire-engines came and in a little while the fires were all put out. The grocer's house was not even touched. Silently, the goblin crept down into the student's room and put the book back on to the table. Then he went back to his cellar and thought about what had happened.

'I'm going to spend one half of the year with the student and the other half with the grocer,' he decided, because, you see, much as he loved the magical tree and the wonderful music, he couldn't quite bring himself to give up the cream and jam.

A ~ Man ~ Among ~ Men

Hausa — West African

There was once a man who had a very good opinion of himself. So wonderful did he think himself that he used to say that he was 'a-man-among-men', meaning that he was brave and superior to everyone else. His wife was always telling him he should be careful. 'Mark my words,' she would say. 'One of these days you are going to meet a real man-among-men, and when you do — well, just you look out.'

Well, one day the boastful man's wife went to the well to fetch water. But the bucket was so heavy that she couldn't pull it up. So she started for home. On the way she met another woman, carrying her small son on her back.

'Why are you coming back with an empty jug?' asked the woman.

'The bucket is too heavy for me to draw up from the well,' replied the boastful man's wife.

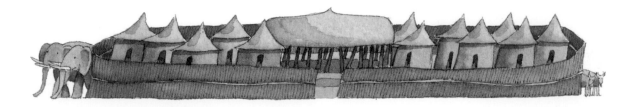

'Oh, just you come with us. We'll get water for you,' said the woman.

So they returned to the well, and the little boy pulled up the bucket as easily as if it were empty.

'What a strong son you have,' said the woman whose husband liked to call himself a-man-among-men.

'Oh, that's nothing compared to his father,' said the boy's mother.

They set off back towards the village and half-way there the woman and her son turned off into the bush.

'Where are you going?' asked the proud man's wife.

'Why, back home,' said the other.

'Whose house do you live in?'

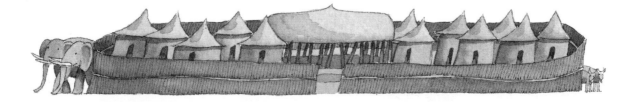

'The house of A-Man-Among-Men, of course,' replied the boy's mother.

When the proud man's wife got home, she told him that she had met a woman whose husband was really called A-Man-Among-Men.

'Ha!' cried the boastful man. 'This I have to see. I'll bet he's not half the man I am.'

Next morning he was the first up. He gathered up his spears and his axe and insisted that his wife take him along to meet A-Man-Among-Men. So they set out and soon arrived at the well. There were the woman and her son just as on the day before.

The boastful man's wife let down the bucket and tried to pull it up. When she could not, the boastful one strutted forward and pulled on the rope. But he couldn't move it either, because he was really a weakling. In fact, the bucket was so heavy that he only got it a few feet up the well-shaft before it fell back, almost pulling him in with it.

The little boy grabbed hold of his foot and saved him from falling. But instead of being grateful the boastful man demanded to be taken to the house of A-Man-Among-Men.

'Very well,' said the boy's mother. 'But don't say I didn't warn you.'

So they set off, and when they reached the place where the ways divided the boastful man's wife refused to go any further. So the foolish man and the woman with the little boy went on together until they reached the house where A-Man-Among-Men lived. But he was not at home, so the woman showed the boastful man where he could hide in the meat-store and watch for her husband returning.

Soon A-Man-Among-Men came back. He was so big that his shadow was at least a mile long. He could eat ten elephants at a time and his voice sounded like a tornado. When the boastful man saw him, he trembled and stayed where he was.

'I smell man,' said A-Man-Among-Men.

'There's no one here but me,' said his wife.

All night the boastful man stayed hidden, and next morning, when the giant went off in search of an elephant for breakfast, he crept out and hurried back towards the village.

He had not gone far before he met A-Man-Among-Men coming home.

'I smell man,' he bellowed, and began to chase the cowardly boaster, who ran off as fast as his legs would carry him.

Soon he came to where some people were clearing the earth.

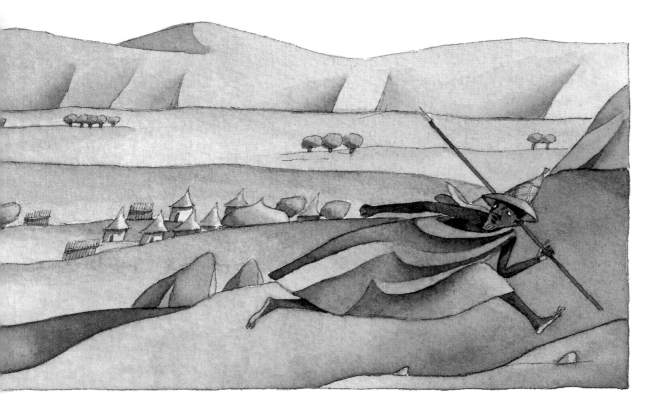

'Why are you running so fast?' one asked him.

'Someone is chasing me,' replied the boastful man.

'Stand here a while, until he comes,' they said. 'Maybe we can help you.'

So the coward stood with them, and in a moment they all felt a rush of wind on their faces.

'What is that?' they asked.

'That is the wind the one chasing me makes as he runs,' said the boastful man.

'Pass on,' said the people, and ran away and hid themselves.

So the boastful man ran on until he came to a place where some people were hoeing the earth.

'Why are you running?' they asked.

'Someone is chasing me,' replied the boastful man.

'Wait until he comes,' they said, 'and maybe we can help you.'

Soon they, too, felt the wind on their faces and when they heard what was causing it they said, 'Pass on,' and ran away to hide. The boastful man ran on again as fast as he could until he came to where a huge man was sitting under a tree. He had an elephant roasting over a fire, and another five lying dead in a heap nearby.

'Why are you running?' asked the huge fellow, whose name was the Giant of the Forest.

'A-Man-Among-Men is after me,' cried the boaster.

'Never heard of him,' said the Giant of the Forest. 'Sit and wait here a while.'

Soon A-Man-Among-Men arrived and the boastful man got up as if to run off.

'Wait!' growled the Giant of the Forest.

'I'm not running away,' cried the coward. 'It's the wind of A-Man-Among-Men that is blowing me away!'

Then the Giant of the Forest began to get angry. He grabbed the boastful man, but at that moment A-Man-Among-Men came up. 'Hey!' he roared. 'That's my bit of a man. Give him to me!'

'Why don't you try and take him?' said the Giant of the Forest.

They began wrestling with each other. So much noise did they make that it sounded like thunder. Then they leapt up into the sky and went on fighting. They were so well-matched that neither could get the better of the other. In fact, they are still up there fighting to this very day, and whenever the people of that land hear thunder in the sky they know it is the two giants fighting.

As for the boastful man, he ran off home, and you can be sure he never called himself 'A-Man-Among-Men' again.

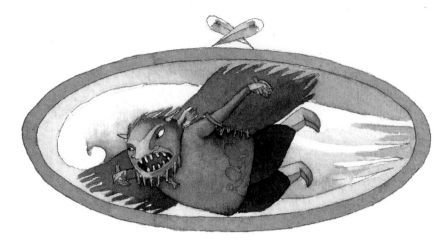

Little Oonyani

Evenk — Siberian

In the Far North there once lived a demon called Korendo. Whenever he got hungry he used to put on a pair of huge wings and fly down to earth in search of people, who he thought tasted better than anything else.

One day Korendo visited a village of the Evenk people. Without warning he swooped down and snatched up everyone he could see, swallowing them all so fast that soon there wasn't a single person left alive — except one old woman, who had hidden under a huge iron cauldron.

At last Korendo flew away and the old woman came out and looked around. At first she thought that she was the only person left and she began to cry. Then she heard a sound.

Hurriedly, the old woman went and searched and, in a corner of one of the tents, she found a baby boy. She brought him out and

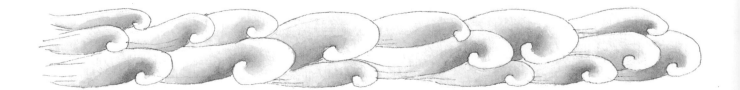

nursed him tenderly and made him a cradle. She named him Oonyani, which means the Lonely One.

The baby grew faster than most, and soon he was a young man. One day he asked the old woman, 'Grandmother, are we the only people in the world?'

'We are indeed,' replied the old woman. And she added, sadly, 'There used to be many more of us, once.'

'What happened to them all?' asked Oonyani.

'The demon Korendo ate them all up,' said the old woman.

Oonyani grew very angry. 'Where does this monster live?' he demanded. 'I will go and kill him.'

'If I knew I would tell you,' answered the old woman, 'but he lives somewhere far away.'

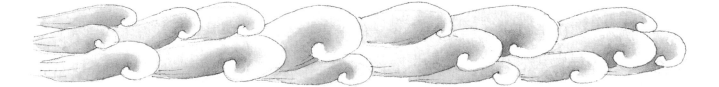

Oonyani was so determined to find the demon that he went out at once into the wild wilderness of the tundra. Soon he was back, with a deer which he had caught.

'Is this Korendo?' he asked.

'No,' answered the old woman. 'That is a gentle deer. It has done you no harm. Let it go at once.'

Oonyani set the deer free, then he went out hunting again. This time he brought back a wolverine.

'Is this Korendo?' he asked.

'No,' answered the old lady. 'That is an innocent beast. Let it go at once!'

Oonyani did as he was told, but the next day he brought back a caribou and a wolf. Again he asked, 'Is this Korendo?' And again the old woman scolded him and made him set the animals free.

The next day, Oonyani brought home a bear, and when that was not Korendo he grew miserable. 'Where shall I look for this demon?' he asked.

'All I know is that he came flying out of the sky,' said the old woman. 'He must live up in the clouds somewhere.'

Oonyani sat and thought for a while. Then he asked the old woman for a broken iron pot. He took a hammer and began to beat the pot. He kept on beating it until he had made himself a pair of splendid wings.

'Now I shall fly up into the clouds and find this monster,' he said.

The old woman shook her head. 'Korendo's wings were much bigger than that.' Oonyani's face fell. Then he set about making the wings bigger. When he had finished he put them on and flew up into the sky. 'Did Korendo fly as high as this?' he asked.

'He flew much higher than that,' said the old woman. 'He was very big and strong.'

Again Oonyani set about making the wings bigger. All day and all night he sat by the fire and hammered away at them until they were bigger than he was. Then he put them on and flew up high into the sky. 'Now am I flying as high as Korendo?' he asked.

'Higher,' said the old woman.

'Good,' said Oonyani, and he flew away at once. As soon as he got in among the clouds he saw a huge tent in the distance. He flew towards it, shouting over and over:

Come out, come out, Korendo,
I've come to take revenge on you!

But the only person who came out was Korendo's wife and she told Oonyani that her husband was not at home. 'You are very foolish to come here,' she told him. 'Korendo is far too strong for you to defeat.'

But Oonyani shook his wings at her and flew on. Soon he saw another great tent pitched amid the clouds and flew towards it. As he arrived he began to shout:

Come out, come out, Korendo,
I've come to take revenge on you.

Now this was indeed Korendo's house, but he was not at home.

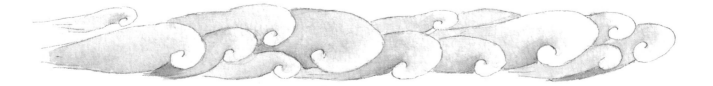

Out came his second wife and looked up at Oonyani. 'You're wasting your time,' she said. 'Korendo is not here, and anyway he's far too strong for you.'

'Tell me where he is,' demanded Oonyani.

'If you really want to find him, you'd better go north,' said Korendo's second wife. 'But don't say I didn't warn you.'

Oonyani flew north until he found another tent and there he met Korendo's third wife, but again the monster was not at home. So Oonyani flew on to a fourth tent and then a fifth and then a sixth.

And at each one he called out his challenge and at each one he was told the same thing: Korendo was not at home and he was too powerful for anyone to defeat, let alone a mere boy.

But Oonyani was determined. He flew on until he came to a seventh tent and hovered outside it, chanting:

Come out, come out, Korendo,
I've come to take revenge on you!

Korendo's seventh wife came out and begged him not to wake the monster. 'For he will surely kill you if you do,' she said. But Oonyani only flew closer to the tent, crying out:

Korendo, Korendo, Korendo,
Come on out and fight me now!

At that Korendo woke up. In a great voice he shouted back, 'Just you wait till I've finished my breakfast!'

'Why bother?' called back Oonyani. 'You won't live much longer.'

'Just wait,' roared Korendo. 'As soon as I put on my boots I'm going to come and eat you!'

'Don't bother with your boots,' called Oonyani. 'You won't need them when you're dead.'

'Just wait while I put on my wings,' bellowed Korendo. 'Then you're for it!'

'Hurry up, then,' shouted Oonyani. 'Or are you afraid to fight me?'

At that, Korendo flew out of his tent with a scream of rage. He flew up towards Oonyani, but the boy simply flew a little higher, so that he was just out of reach. Up and up, higher and higher, they flew. Soon Korendo was breathless and began to get tired. 'Come here,' he bellowed. 'Let me get at you!'

But Oonyani went higher still. Then, when Korendo was groaning and gasping for air, he flew down and landed on the monster's back. With a single wrench, Oonyani broke off one of Korendo's wings.

With a cry, the demon fell out of the sky. Down and down and down he fell, until he hit the ground and broke into pieces. Out of his insides came all the people he had eaten, alive and well. Everyone from Oonyani's village was there, and when they saw the boy they were overjoyed. He led them all back to where the old woman waited, and so thankful were they that they made Oonyani their leader.

Korendo's seven wives came and gathered up all the pieces and burned them. It was said that the smoke from the demon's funeral pyre could be seen for seven hundred miles. As for Oonyani, he had many more adventures and lived to a great age.

The Lass Who Couldn't Be Frightened

Scottish

There was once a lass who couldn't be frightened. Her mother was dead and her father had run off no one knew where, so apart from a cat and dog, the lass lived all alone in a house in the depths of the forest. People used to say to her that she ought to come and live in the village with them, but she would just shrug her shoulders and say, 'I have my cat and my dog for company.'

'But what about the wild animals in the forest?' the people asked.

'I'm not afraid of them,' said the lass.

'Well, what about the wee folk?' the people said, looking left and right and back and forward and up and down as they did so, and dropping their voices to a whisper.

'Och, those are just goodwives' tales,' said the lass, with a laugh.

The villagers looked at each other and shrugged. If the lass was foolish enough not to believe in the wee folk that was her look-out.

Then one day one of the village lads took a look at the lass and realised she was the best-looking girl for miles. He took another look and thought he might like to marry her. He talked about this idea to some of his friends and within a week or two there was a queue of lads outside her gate with bunches of flowers and silly smiles on their faces. But the lass sent them all away. 'Why should I be wanting to get married?' she said. 'I have everything I need here and my dog is the best protection. Now be off with you all!'

But there was one lad who didn't go with the rest, and that was Hughie the shepherd boy. When the others pointed out what a bonny girl the lass was he just said, 'Aye, I've noticed.' Then he went back to his sheep. The other lads thought he was just plain daft, but they soon got tired of getting nowhere with the lass, and after a time they all left her alone.

Now, one evening the lass went out to the meal-bin to get some meal to make bannocks for her supper. 'Och,' she said. 'After I've filled this bowl there'll be nothing left to make porridge in the morning.' And she thought to herself that it was a fine night and that she might as well take a sack of grain to be ground by the miller. So off she went, but by the time she reached the mill it was dark and the mill was all closed up. But the lass saw that there were lights on in the miller's house, so she went and knocked at the door.

The miller came and stuck his head around the door and glared at her.

'I'm sorry to trouble you this late, but I have a bag of grain to be ground. Would you be kind and do it for me?'

'I will not,' snapped the miller. 'Come back in the morning.'

'But I need meal to make porridge for breakfast,' said the lass.

'Well, you'll have to wait,' said the miller, and started to close the door.

'Will you give me the key to the mill and let me do it myself?' said the lass.

'No, I will not,' shouted the miller, going red in the face.

'And why not?' demanded the lass.

'If you must know,' said the miller, 'there's a terrible great goblin that lives under the mill, and if anyone tries to grind any flour at night he comes out and steals it and gives them a good thrashing into the bargain.'

'Well, I'm not frightened of any silly goblin,' said the lass, who was beginning to get angry herself. 'Give me the key.'

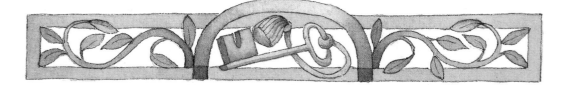

When he saw that she wouldn't be put off, the miller called his wife and his children to witness that he was not to blame for anything that might happen, then he gave the lass the key to the mill and went indoors and bolted the door and barred the windows.

The lass went right into the mill and put her grain into the hopper and set the huge mill-wheel turning. Almost at once a great big goblin with an ugly face and huge great staring eyes came bursting up out of the floor and tried to snatch the lass's bag of meal. He had a big knobbly club in one hand, but when she saw him the lass was not a bit afraid. She snatched the club out of the goblin's hand and set about him with it.

Now the goblin wasn't used to this kind of treatment. In the past he had only to appear and everyone in the mill would run away screaming. The lass was a different kettle of fish. She boxed his ears and banged his shins and chased him into one corner and then another until his head was in a whirl.

Then, as he was passing the hopper the lass gave him a great big kick, and he fell right into the bin. The lass started up the mill-wheel and there the goblin was, between the mill-wheels, getting ground up with all the grain.

Of course, it didn't kill him because almost nothing can kill a goblin, but he yelled and made such a racket that it sounded as though a dozen folk were being murdered. The miller and his family pulled the bedclothes over their heads and shivered with fright, but the lass just sat down and listened to the goblin calling to her to let him out.

'You just stay there for a bit,' she said. 'It will do you good.'

'Och,' said the goblin. 'Please let me out. I promise to go away and never to bother anyone again.'

'Do you now?' said the lass.

'I do, so,' said the goblin.

So the lass let him out and the goblin ran off as fast as he could and was never seen again in those parts.

The lass went and banged on the miller's door. It was a while before he got up the courage to come down. The lass gave him back the key to the mill. 'There,' she said. 'I've ground my grain and I've got rid of your goblin, and now I'm off home.'

Next day the story was all over the village. When Hughie the shepherd boy heard it he went very quiet, for in his heart he had loved the lass for a long time, and he'd thought that one day she might change her mind about needing a man to protect her. But after this adventure it seemed as though he was wrong.

On his way home he happened to pass near the house in the forest where the lass lived. There he heard something that made his hair stand on end — it was the voice of the lass screaming and crying fit to burst. 'It must be a band of robbers that are after her,' thought Hughie, and he set off at a run towards the lass's house.

When he got there he found the door standing wide open. Inside the lass was standing on the table, screaming loud enough to wake the dead. And there at her feet was a wee brown mouse.

'I thought you were the lass who was afraid of nothing,' said Hughie.

The lass opened her eyes and stopped screeching. 'Och, Hughie, get rid of that beastie for me. The cat's in the fields and the dog's away hunting, and no one can save me but you!'

'Looks to me like you could use a man about the place,' said Hughie.

'Maybe I could, at that,' said the lass.

So Hughie took the broom from behind the door and chased the mouse away. Then he helped the lass down from the table and gave her a big hug and an even bigger kiss.

'We'll be married on Sunday,' he said. And the lass said, quietly as anything, 'Aye, let's.'

And married they were, and lived happily for the rest of their days, and the lass never was afraid of anything — except maybe mice, but she had Hughie to take care of them.

Sources

The Giant with No Heart in His Body
This is one of the most famous Norwegian stories collected by Peter Christian Asbjornsen in the nineteenth century. It is told in several other Scandinavian countries and there is even a version from Scotland. I found it in a wonderful collection called *Scandinavian Folk and Fairy Tales* edited by Clair Boss (Avenal Books, London, 1984).

The Ghost with Two Faces
This story comes from the Cheyenne people of North America. It was first taken down by the great collector of stories Alfred L. Kroeber, and published in *The Journal of American Folk-Lore* in the year 1900. Hunt-the-Plum-Pit must be the oldest game in the world, and crops up again in just about every culture in such games as Find-the-Lady and Spot-the-Shell.

The Bunyip
This is a favourite story from Australia which I found years ago in one of Andrew Lang's great collections of fairy tales. It has a wry sense of humour which I love — especially the way the men all try to dodge the work their wives have given them to do!

Oona and the Giant
This is a famous story which is told all over Ireland. Both Fionn mac Cool and Cuchulainn were famous heroes who grew into giants over the years as the stories about them got taller. The version here is retold from a collection made by Campbell of Islay in 1827.

The Drinking Companions
This wonderful little ghost story is from China, where the belief still holds that when you die you are reborn into another body, according to how good or bad you have been. This tale comes from a collection called *Chinese Fairy Tales and Fantasies* by Moss Roberts (Pantheon Books, New York, 1979). My own version is a free adaptation of this.

The Goblin, the Grocer and the Student
This story is based on one from the pen of the great Scandinavian story-teller, Hans Christian Andersen, who is probably best known for his tale of 'The Little Mermaid'. I remember reading it years ago in Andrew Lang's *Pink Fairy Book* (Longmans, London, 1897), and it is on his translation that I have based this version.

A-Man-Among-Men
This story comes from the Hausa people of West Africa. Many of these stories were collected by a man named Frank Edga and written in the original language. They were translated by Neil Skinner in a book called *Hausa Tales and Traditions* (Africana Publishing Co., New York, 1973). My own version is freely adapted from this.

Little Oonyani
This story is from the Evenk tribe of the Eskimo people in what is really a part of Siberia. I found it in an old book of *Stories of the Far North*, and it has also been retold by James Riordan in his wonderful book *The Sun Maiden and the Crescent Moon* (Canongate, Edinburgh, 1989).

The Lass Who Couldn't Be Frightened
This wonderful tale is an old story told by the wandering seanachies (story-tellers) from the Durris area of Scotland. I found it in a collection called *Thistle & Thyme* by Sorche Nic Leodhas (Bodley Head, London, 1965). I have made free use of this as all story-tellers will and made my own version.

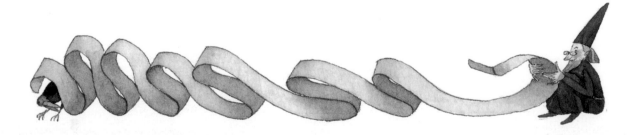

BAREFOOT BOOKS publishes high-quality picture
books for children of all ages and specialises in the work of
artists and writers from many cultures. If you have enjoyed
this book and would like to receive a copy of our current
catalogue, please contact our London office —
tel: 0171 704 6492   fax: 0171 359 5798
e-mail: sales@barefoot-books.com
website: www.barefoot-books.com